CW01024475

Bathmania
How To Make Bath Bombs, Bath Salts & Bubble Baths
53 All Natural & Organic Recipes

All contents copyrighted © 2015 of Lorraine White. All rights reserved worldwide. No part of this publication may be reproduced in any form or by any means, including scanning, photocopying, or otherwise without prior written permission of the copyright holder.

In no event shall the author be liable for any direct, indirect, incidental, punitive or consequential damages of any kind whatsoever with respect to the service, the materials and the products contained within. This book is not a substitute for professional medical or skin care advice.

Table of Contents

	Page
Introduction	2
Bath Bomb Recipes – A few notes	3
Avocado Bath Bombs	4
Grapefruit Bath Bombs	5
Orange Bath Bombs	6
Lemon Bath Bombs	7
Ylang Ylang Bath Bombs	8
Stress Relief Bath Bombs	9
Goodnight Bath Bombs	10
Cold Relief Bath Bombs	11
Aching Joints Bath Bombs	12
Cool Coconut Bath Bombs	13
Straight To Sleep Bath Bombs	14
Basic Bath Bombs	16
Lush Bath Bombs	17
Lavender Bath Bombs	18
Tea Tree Bath Bombs	19
Soft Skin Bath Bombs	20
Oatmeal Bath Bombs	21
Peppermint Bath Bombs	22
Bath Salts Recipes – A few notes	23
Woody Scent Bath Salts	24
Lavender Rose Bath Salts	25
Balancing Bath Salts	26
Lemon & Basil Bath Salts	27
Almond & Peppermint Bath Salts	28
Custom Bath Salts	29
Musky Jasmine Bath Salts	30
Organic Detox Bath Salts	31
Earthy Bath Salts	32

Sensual Summer Bath Salts	33
Tea Tree Bath Salts	34
Rejuvenating Bath Salts	35
Honey Bath Salts	36
Milky Bath Salts	37
Bay Leaf & Mint Bath Salts	38
Deep Soak Bath Salts	39
Ocean Fresh Bath Salts	40
Citrus Bath Salts	41
Pretty Peach Bath Salts	42
Uplifting Bath Salts	43
Heavy Head Bath Salts	44
Lemongrass & Cinnamon Bath Salts	45
Lemon Fizz Bath Salts	46
Toxin Exterminator Bath Salts	47
Bubble Bath Recipes – A few notes	48
Cherry Bubble Bath	49
Bergamot & Lime Bubble Bath	50
Lavender Bubble Bath	51
Honey & Vanilla Bubble Bath	52
Rosemary Milk Bath	53
Milk & Honey Bubble Bath	54
Raspberry Bubble Bath	55
Rose Bubble Bath	56
Herb & Oil Bubble Bath	57
Jasmine Delight Bubble Bath	58
Apple Bubble Bath	59
Conclusion	60
My Other Homemade Beauty Product Books	61

You may like my other books in this series, all available on Amazon

Homemade Body Scrubs : 52 All Natural And Easy To Make Body Scrubs, Face Masks, Lip Balms And Body Washes

Homemade Lotion : 41 All Natural Simple And Easy To Make Body Lotions, Body Butters and Lotion Bars

How To Be Beautiful With Homemade Beauty Products. Over 50 Organic Face Masks, Face Cleansers & Face Creams

Homemade Shampoo: Make Your Own Organic & Natural Hair Products For Luscious Hair

Homemade Foot Spa: 48 All Natural Foot Soak, Foot Scrubs, Foot Creams & Heel Balm Recipes

Homemade Deodorant: 32 Simple Organic DIY Recipes For Making Natural Deodorants & Body Sprays

Introduction

Hello and welcome,

My name is Lorraine White and I am a wife and mother to three wonderful children. I am like most moms who juggle work and home life. About five years ago I started to make my own natural beauty products after I learned about some of the damaging and toxic chemicals that some manufacturers put in the products that we buy in the store.

In this book, I am giving you **53** of the best **Homemade Bath Bombs, Bath Salts & Bubble Bath recipes.**

What makes all these recipes fabulous is how quickly you can put these together. Once you have bought a few basic ingredients then you will be able to make lots of these bath-time products not only for you and your family, but for friends and colleagues too.

There is nothing better than going **NATURAL**. When you make your products, you know **EXACTLY** what is in them and you can make up batches of recipes dependent on how you are feeling.

The sky is the limit when it comes to making your own natural beauty products. You are only limited by your own imagination. Anything is possible. Are you ready to learn how to make the most luxurious bath-time products? Yes? Then let us begin!

Lorraine xx

Bath Bomb Recipes

Bath bombs are wonderful. Simply drop one (or two or three) into your bath water and watch it fizz into action. You can relax and pamper yourself in a luxurious bath with natural organic ingredients that have been proven to be good for your skin.

Depending on the quality of the oils, herbs and salts you use, you can create some amazing bath bombs. The benefits of these products are immense.

Epsom salts, dead sea salts and baking soda are used in these recipes because they help to detoxify and release the toxins in your skin and the oils are used to relieve tension and aid relaxation. Try some of the recipes, you will love them.

A few notes:

- The recipes in the bath bomb section make between 5-10 bath bombs.
- You can use any mold you like for your bath bombs but try to keep it simple to avoid cracking and breakage of your bath bombs.
- Muffin pans/tins work great for bath bombs (gently oil the individual sections first) as do silicone molds or plastic egg molds that you can buy from craft stores.
- You can mix and match salts (dead sea salts, Epsom salts, rock salt etc.) and you can also use your favorite essential oils and carrier oils (jasmine, jojoba, grapeseed, vegetable, olive oil etc.)
- You can add dried herbs and flowers to your bath bombs to add interest
- Adding liquid food coloring is optional
- Add 1 – 3 bath bombs to your water when you are ready to use them

Avocado Bath Bombs

What you need:

- 2 tbs. citric acid
- 2 tbs. cornstarch
- 1/4 cup baking soda
- 3 tbs. avocado oil
- 1/4 tsp. fragrance oil
- 3-6 drops of food coloring (optional)
- Paper candy cups

How to make them:

1. Place all of the dry ingredients (first 3) into a bowl and mix well.
2. Place avocado oil into a small glass bowl and add fragrance oil and food coloring if you are using it
3. Slowly add oil mixture into dry ingredients and mix well.
4. Scoop up small amounts of the mixture and shape into 1" balls.
5. Let the balls rest on a sheet of waxed paper for about 2 to 3 hours, then place each ball into a candy cup to let dry and harden for 24 to 48 hours.
6. Store bombs in a closed, air-tight container.

Grapefruit Bath Bombs

What you need:

- Stainless Steel Bath Bomb Mold
- 16 oz. Citric Acid
- 32 oz. Baking Soda
- 75 oz. Pink Grapefruit Fragrance Oil
- Witch Hazel
- 3 tablespoons Red Mica

How to make them:

1. Combine the citric acid and baking soda in a large bowl and mix well. Use your fingers to break up any clumps.
2. Once the mixture is smooth, add the red mica and mix well until you have a soft pink color. Once thoroughly mixed in, add your fragrance oil.
3. Spritz with witch hazel (about 6 spritzes) until the mixture is slightly firm
4. Fill each half of the mold and pack mixture as tight as you can.
5. Sprinkle on a little extra and place the second half of the mold on top.
6. To avoid cracking, squeeze the two halves together as hard as you can.
7. Let the mixture rest in the mold for about 30 seconds then carefully slide it out of the mold onto a flat surface.
8. Let them dry, undisturbed until fully hardened.

Orange Bath Bombs

What you need:

Dry ingredients

- 1 cup baking soda
- ½ cup citric acid
- ½ cup corn starch
- 1/3 cup Epsom salts

Wet ingredients

- 2 ½ tablespoons grapeseed oil
- ¾ tablespoon water
- 15 drops orange essential oil
- 1 teaspoon vitamin E oil
- 8 drops orange liquid food coloring
- Witch hazel in a spray bottle

How to make them:

1. Combine first three ingredients in a sifter and sift together until smooth
2. Add Epsom salts and set aside
3. Combine all wet ingredients together and add this mixture to the dry ingredients
4. Spritz a little with witch hazel
5. Press mixture into molds of your choice making sure the mixture is packed very tightly
6. Allow bath bombs to dry overnight
7. Remove from molds and store in an air-tight container

Lemon Bath Bombs

What you need:

Dry ingredients

- 1 cup baking soda
- ½ cup citric acid
- ½ cup corn starch
- 1/3 cup Epsom salts

Wet ingredients

- 2 ½ tablespoons sweet almond oil
- ¾ tablespoon water
- 20 drops lemon essential oil
- 8 drops yellow liquid food coloring
- Witch hazel in a spray bottle

How to make them:

1. Combine first three ingredients in a sifter and sift together until smooth
2. Add Epsom salts and set aside
3. Combine all wet ingredients together and add this mixture to the dry ingredients
4. Spritz a little with witch hazel
5. Press mixture into molds of your choice making sure the mixture is packed very tightly
6. Allow bath bombs to dry overnight
7. Remove from molds and store in an air-tight container

Ylang Ylang Bath Bombs

What you need:

Dry ingredients

- 1 cup baking soda
- ½ cup citric acid
- ½ cup corn starch
- 1/3 cup Epsom salts

Wet ingredients

- 2 ½ tablespoons grapeseed oil
- ¾ tablespoon water
- 20 drops ylang ylang essential oil
- 1 teaspoon vitamin E oil
- 8 drops yellow liquid food coloring
- Witch hazel in a spray bottle

How to make them:

1. Combine first three ingredients in a sifter and sift together until smooth
2. Add Epsom salts and set aside
3. Combine all wet ingredients together and add this mixture to the dry ingredients
4. Spritz a little with witch hazel
5. Press mixture into molds of your choice making sure the mixture is packed very tightly
6. Allow bath bombs to dry overnight
7. Remove from molds and store in an air-tight container

Stress Relief Bath Bombs

What you need:

Dry ingredients

- 1 cup baking soda
- ½ cup citric acid
- ½ cup corn starch
- 1/3 cup Epsom salts

Wet ingredients

- 2 ½ tablespoons almond oil
- ¾ tablespoon water
- 15 drops lavender essential oil
- 5 drops ylang ylang essential oil
- 10 drops petitgrain essential oil
- 8 drops liquid food coloring
- Witch hazel in a spray bottle

How to make them:

1. Combine first three ingredients in a sifter and sift together until smooth
2. Add Epsom salts and set aside
3. Combine all wet ingredients together and add this mixture to the dry ingredients
4. Spritz a little with witch hazel (about 6 spritzes)
5. Press mixture into molds of your choice making sure the mixture is packed very tightly
6. Allow bath bombs to dry overnight

Goodnight Bath Bombs

What you need:

Dry ingredients

- 1 cup baking soda
- ½ cup citric acid
- ½ cup corn starch
- 1/3 cup Epsom salts

Wet ingredients

- 2 ½ tablespoons almond oil
- ¾ tablespoon water
- 2 tablespoons dried lavender
- 2 tablespoons dried chamomile
- 5 drops chamomile essential oil
- 15 drops lavender essential oil
- 8 drops liquid food coloring
- Witch hazel in a spray bottle

How to make them:

1. Combine first three ingredients in a sifter and sift together until smooth
2. Add Epsom salts and set aside
3. Combine all wet ingredients together and add this mixture to the dry ingredients
4. Spritz a little with witch hazel (about 6 spritzes)
5. Press mixture into molds of your choice making sure the mixture is packed very tightly
6. Allow bath bombs to dry overnight

Cold Relief Bath Bombs

What you need:

Dry ingredients

- 1 cup baking soda
- ½ cup citric acid
- ½ cup corn starch
- 1/3 cup Epsom salts

Wet ingredients

- 2 ½ tablespoons olive oil
- ¾ tablespoon water
- 5 drops eucalyptus essential oil
- 5 drops lavender essential oil
- 5 drops marjoram essential oil
- 3 drops tea tree essential oil
- 8 drops liquid food coloring
- Witch hazel in a spray bottle

How to make them:

1. Combine first three ingredients in a sifter and sift together until smooth
2. Add Epsom salts and set aside
3. Combine all wet ingredients together and add this mixture to the dry ingredients
4. Spritz a little with witch hazel (about 6 spritzes)
5. Press mixture into molds of your choice making sure the mixture is packed very tightly
6. Allow bath bombs to dry overnight

Aching Joints Bath Bombs

What you need:

Dry ingredients

- 1 cup baking soda
- ½ cup citric acid
- ½ cup corn starch
- 1/3 cup Epsom salts

Wet ingredients

- 2 ½ tablespoons grapeseed oil
- ¾ tablespoon water
- 5 drops white birch essential oil
- 5 drops ginger essential oil
- 5 drops juniper essential oil
- 5 drops marjoram essential oil
- 5 drops rosemary essential oil
- 8 drops liquid food coloring
- Witch hazel in a spray bottle

How to make them:

1. Combine first three ingredients in a sifter and sift together until smooth
2. Add Epsom salts and set aside
3. Combine all wet ingredients together and add this mixture to the dry ingredients
4. Spritz a little with witch hazel (about 6 spritzes)
5. Press mixture into molds of your choice making sure the mixture is packed very tightly

6. Allow bath bombs to dry overnight

Cool Coconut Bath Bombs

What you need:

Dry ingredients

- 1 cup baking soda
- ½ cup citric acid
- ½ cup corn starch
- 1/3 cup Epsom salts

Wet ingredients

- 2 ½ tablespoons olive oil
- ¾ tablespoon water
- ¼ teaspoon coconut fragrance oil
- 1 teaspoon vitamin E oil
- 8 drops liquid food coloring
- Witch hazel in a spray bottle

How to make them:

1. Combine first three ingredients in a sifter and sift together until smooth
2. Add Epsom salts and set aside
3. Combine all wet ingredients together and add this mixture to the dry ingredients
4. Spritz a little with witch hazel (about 6 spritzes)
5. Press mixture into molds of your choice making sure the mixture is packed very tightly
6. Allow bath bombs to dry overnight

Straight To Sleep Bath Bombs

What you need:

Dry ingredients

- 1 cup baking soda
- ½ cup citric acid
- ½ cup corn starch
- 1/3 cup Epsom salts

Wet ingredients

- 2 ½ tablespoons grapeseed oil
- ¾ tablespoon water
- 5 drops chamomile essential oil
- 5 drops lavender essential oil
- 5 drops orange essential oil
- 5 drops tangerine essential oil
- 5 drops marjoram essential oil
- 5 drops ylang ylang essential oil
- 8 drops liquid food coloring
- Witch hazel in a spray bottle

How to make them:

1. Combine first three ingredients in a sifter and sift together until smooth
2. Add Epsom salts and set aside
3. Combine all wet ingredients together and add this mixture to the dry ingredients
4. Spritz a little with witch hazel (about 6 spritzes)

5. Press mixture into molds of your choice making sure the mixture is packed very tightly
6. Allow bath bombs to dry overnight

Basic Bath Bombs

What you need:

Dry ingredients

- 1 cup baking soda
- ½ cup citric acid
- ½ cup corn starch
- 1/3 cup Epsom salts

Wet ingredients

- 2 ½ tablespoons jojoba oil
- ¾ tablespoon water
- 5 drops lavender essential oil
- 5 drops marjoram essential oil
- ¼ cup fresh lavender sprigs
- 8 drops liquid food coloring
- Witch hazel in a spray bottle

How to make them:

1. Combine first three ingredients in a sifter and sift together until smooth
2. Add Epsom salts and set aside
3. Combine all wet ingredients together and add this mixture to the dry ingredients
4. Spritz a little with witch hazel (about 6 spritzes)
5. Press mixture into molds of your choice making sure the mixture is packed very tightly
6. Allow bath bombs to dry overnight

Lush Bath Bombs

What you need:

Dry ingredients

- 1 cup baking soda
- ½ cup citric acid
- ½ cup corn starch
- 1/3 cup Epsom salts

Wet ingredients

- 2 ½ tablespoons grapeseed oil
- ¾ tablespoon water
- 5 drops ylang ylang essential oil
- 5 drops juniper essential oil
- 5 drops chamomile essential oil
- 5 drops rosemary essential oil
- 8 drops liquid food coloring
- Witch hazel in a spray bottle

How to make them:

1. Combine first three ingredients in a sifter and sift together until smooth
2. Add Epsom salts and set aside
3. Combine all wet ingredients together and add this mixture to the dry ingredients
4. Spritz a little with witch hazel (about 6 spritzes)
5. Press mixture into molds of your choice making sure the mixture is packed very tightly
6. Allow bath bombs to dry overnight

Lavender Bath Bombs

What you need:

- 5-6 fresh lavender sprigs
- 1 tbsp. citric acid powder
- 3 tbsp. bicarbonate of soda
- 10 drops lavender essential oil
- 1 teaspoon almond oil
- Biscuit cutters (to use as a molds) or any mold of your choice

How to make them:

1. Mix the citric acid and bicarbonate of soda together
2. Add the lavender essential oil and the lavender sprigs
3. Add almond oil and mix together well
4. Place a biscuit cutter on the top of a sheet of baking paper
5. Add the mixture to the biscuit cutters or molds
6. Pack the mixture tightly inside the biscuit cutters or molds
7. Allow bath bombs to dry overnight

Tea Tree Bath Bombs

What you need:

- 1 cup baking soda
- 1 cup citric acid
- ½ cup cornstarch
- ½ cup jojoba oil
- 10 drops tea tree essential oil
- 8 drops liquid food coloring
- Plastic egg molds or a muffin tray

How to make them:

1. Combine all the ingredients together in a bowl
2. Pack the mixture tightly inside the egg molds or muffin tray
3. Allow bath bombs to dry overnight and remove gently
4. Add one of the bombs to your bath

Soft Skin Bath Bombs

What you need:

- 1 ½ cups bicarbonate of soda
- ½ cup citric acid
- ¼ cup lavender sprigs
- 10 drops lavender essential oil
- 5 drops geranium
- 1 teaspoon almond oil
- 8 drops liquid food coloring
- Any molds of your choice

How to make them:

1. Mix the citric acid and bicarbonate of soda together
2. Add the lavender sprigs
3. In another bowl combine the almond oil, essential oils and food coloring
4. Add more food coloring if you want a deeper color
5. Work the mixture in your hands and press into the molds
6. Make sure the mixture is packed very tightly
7. Allow bath bombs to dry overnight
8. Drop a bath bomb into hot bath water
9. Relax and enjoy it

Oatmeal Bath Bombs

What you need:

- ¼ cup baking soda
- ¼ cup oatmeal
- 2 tablespoons citric acid
- 2 tablespoons cornstarch
- 2 tablespoons jojoba oil
- 2 tablespoons water
- 8 drops liquid food coloring (optional)
- 10 drops rose essential oil
- Any molds of your choice (you can even use a muffin tin)

How to make them:

1. Combine baking soda, oatmeal, citric acid and cornstarch in a bowl
2. Add jojoba oil, rose essential oil and food coloring if using it
3. Mix until well combined
4. If the mixture is too dry, add a few drops of water
5. Press the mixture firmly into the molds
6. Allow bath bombs to dry overnight

Peppermint Bath Bombs

What you need:

- ¼ cup baking soda
- 2 tablespoons citric acid
- 2 tablespoons cornstarch
- 2 tablespoons coconut oil
- 2 tablespoons water
- 15 drops peppermint oil
- 8 drops liquid food coloring (optional)
- 10 drops rose essential oil
- Any molds of your choice (you can even use a muffin tin)

How to make them:

1. Combine baking soda, citric acid and cornstarch in a bowl
2. Add coconut oil, rose essential oil and food coloring if using it
3. Mix until well combined
4. If the mixture is too dry, add a few drops of water
5. Press the mixture firmly into the molds
6. Allow bath bombs to dry overnight
7. Store them in air-tight containers
8. Drop one into a hot bath when you are ready to use them

Bath Salts Recipes

Adding natural organic bath salts to your bath can take it from ordinary to amazingly luxurious. Every time you have a bath, pour some of these wonderful bath salts into it for a spa like experience.

Depending on the quality of the oils, herbs and salts you use, you can create some amazing bath salt recipes. The benefits of these products are immense.

Epsom salts, dead sea salts and baking soda are used in these recipes because they help to detoxify and release the toxins in your skin and the oils are used to relieve tension and aid relaxation. Try some of the recipes, you will love them.

A few notes:

- I've mixed and matched recipes in this section with recipes for just one bath and recipes for up to 4 baths
- They are so easy to make, there's no need making more than you need, that way it stays fresh and you get maximum health benefits from the properties of the oils, herbs and salts
- You can add dried herbs and flowers to your bath salts to add interest
- You can mix and match the salts, herbs and essential oils that I use, use what you like, it is your recipe.
- Adding liquid food coloring is optional
- These bath salts are great to give away as gifts
- You can add extra interest by using different colored food coloring, simply separate your salts into sections and add the different food coloring to each section.
- You can grind the bath salts in a food processor if you want an even finer bath salt.
- Experiment and enjoy yourself.

Woody Scent Bath Salts

What you need:

- 1 cup dead sea salt
- 1 cup Epsom salts
- 2 tablespoons baking soda
- 5 drops rosewood essential oil
- 5 drops cedarwood essential oil
- 3 drops chamomile essential oil
- Air tight jar

How to make it:

1. Combine baking soda, dead sea salt and Epsom salt in a bowl and mix well
2. In a cup, mix the oils together
3. Pour the oils over the dry ingredients and mix together well
4. Allow the scents to infuse by leaving it to sit for 2 hours
5. Store in an air-tight jar
6. Add to your bath as and when you feel like it

Lavender Rose Bath Salts

What you need:

- 1 cup sea salt
- 3 tablespoons baking soda
- 5 drops lavender essential oil
- 5 drops rose essential oil
- Air tight jar

How to make it:

1. Add all ingredients to the jar and shake vigorously to mix well
2. Allow the scents to infuse by leaving it to sit for 2 hours
3. Put it in your air tight jar
4. Add to your running bath and enjoy

Balancing Bath Salts

What you need:

- 1 cup epsom salt
- 2 tablespoons sea salt
- 3 tablespoons baking soda
- 5 drops bergamot essential oil
- 5 drops frankincense essential oil
- 2 drops geranium essential oil
- Air tight jar

How to make it:

1. Add all ingredients to the jar and shake vigorously to mix well
2. Allow the scents to infuse by leaving it to sit for 2 hours
3. Put it in your air tight jar
4. Add to your running bath and enjoy

Lemon & Basil Bath Salts

What you need:

- 1 ½ cups epsom salt
- 2 tablespoons sea salt
- 3 tablespoons baking soda
- 5 drops lemon scented oil
- 5 drops basil oil
- 2 drops green liquid food coloring
- 2 drops yellow liquid food coloring
- Air tight jar

How to make it:

1. Combine the Epsom salt, sea salt and baking powder in a bowl
2. Mix all other ingredients in another bowl
3. Add the wet mixture to the dry mixture and make sure you combine it together well
4. Put the mixture in your air tight jar
5. Allow the scents to infuse by leaving it to sit for 2 hours
6. Add to your running bath and enjoy

Almond & Peppermint Bath Salts

What you need:

- 1 ½ cups epsom salt
- 2 tablespoons sea salt
- 3 tablespoons baking soda
- 3 teaspoons sweet almond oil
- 10 drops peppermint essential oil
- 2 drops green liquid food coloring
- Air tight jar

How to make it:

1. Combine the Epsom salt, sea salt and baking powder in a bowl
2. Mix all other ingredients in another bowl
3. Add the wet mixture to the dry mixture and make sure you combine it together well
4. Put the mixture in your air tight jar
5. Allow the scents to infuse by leaving it to sit for 2 hours
6. Add to your running bath and enjoy

Custom Bath Salts

What you need:

- 1 ½ cups rock salt
- 2 tablespoons sea salt
- 10 drops of your favorite essential oil
- Air tight jar

How to make it:

1. Put all ingredients in your air tight jar and shake vigorously to mix together well
2. Allow the scents to infuse by leaving it to sit for 2 hours
3. Add to your running bath and enjoy

Musky Jasmine Bath Salts

What you need:

- 1 cup baking soda
- 3 cups sea salt
- 4 drops musk oil
- 5 drops jasmine essential oil
- 2 tablespoons glycerin
- 2 drops liquid food coloring
- Air tight jar

How to make it:

1. Combine the sea salt and baking soda in a bowl
2. Mix all other ingredients in another bowl
3. Add the wet mixture to the dry mixture and make sure you combine it together well
4. Pour the mixture into your air tight container
5. Allow the scents to infuse by leaving it to sit for 2 hours
6. Add to your running bath and enjoy

Organic Detox Bath Salts

What you need:

- 2 handfuls Epsom salts
- 1 handful sea salt
- 2 teaspoons sweet almond oil
- 8 drops rosemary essential oil

How to make it:

1. Put all ingredients in a hot running bath tub
2. Place your body in the bath tub
3. Relax and enjoy the detoxifying feeling

Earthy Bath Salts

What you need:

- ½ cup epsom salts
- ¾ cup baking soda
- ½ cup sea salt
- 2 teaspoons almond oil
- 20 drops patchouli essential oil
- 15 drops rose essential oil
- 2 drops green liquid food coloring
- Air tight jar

How to make it:

1. Put the mixture in your air tight jar and shake vigorously
2. Allow the scents to infuse by leaving it to sit for 2 hours
3. Add to your running bath and enjoy

Sensual Summer Bath Salts

What you need:

- 1 ½ cups epsom salt
- ¼ cup liquid ivory soap
- 2 teaspoons olive oil
- 4 drops chamomile essential oil
- 4 drops juniper essential oil
- 2 drops liquid food coloring
- Air tight jar

How to make it:

1. Put all ingredients in your air tight jar and shake vigorously to mix together well
2. Allow the scents to infuse by leaving it to sit for 2 hours
3. Add to your running bath and enjoy

Tea Tree Bath Salts

What you need:

- 3 tablespoons sea salt
- 3 tablespoons baking soda
- 8 drops tea tree essential oil
- Air tight jar

How to make it:

1. Put all the ingredients in your air tight jar and shake it vigorously to mix together well
2. Allow the scents to infuse by leaving it to sit for 2 hours
3. Add to your running bath and enjoy

Rejuvenating Bath Salts

What you need:

- 1 cup sea salt
- 1 tablespoon baking soda
- 3 drops bergamot essential oil
- 3 drops rose essential oil
- 3 drops lavender essential oil
- 3 drops frankincense essential oil
- Air tight jar

How to make it:

1. Put all dry ingredients in a bowl and mix together well
2. Put all wet ingredients in another bowl and mix together well
3. Add the wet ingredients to the dry ingredients and mix together well
4. Pour the mixture into your air tight jar and shake vigorously to combine
5. Allow the scents to infuse by leaving it to sit for 2 hours
6. Add to your running bath and enjoy

Honey Bath Salts

What you need:

- 1 ½ cups rock salt
- 1/3 cup liquid (runny) honey
- 2 drops yellow liquid food coloring
- 3 drops lemon essential oil
- 3 drops jasmine essential oil
- Air tight jar

How to make it:

1. Combine the rock salt and honey in a bowl and mix together well
2. Add liquid food coloring and essential oils
3. Pour the mixture into your air tight jar and shake vigorously to combine
4. Allow the scents to infuse by leaving it to sit for 2 hours
5. Add to your running bath and enjoy

Milky Bath Salts

What you need:

- 1 ½ cups sea salt
- 1 cup Epsom salts
- 3 cups powdered milk
- 10 drops vanilla
- 5 drops sweet orange essential oil
- 5 drops rose essential oil
- Air tight jar

How to make it:

1. Put all ingredients in the air tight jar and shake vigorously to combine all ingredients
2. Make sure they are mixed together well
3. Allow the scents to infuse by leaving it to sit for 2 hours
4. Add to your running bath and enjoy

Bay Leaf & Mint Bath Salts

What you need:

- ½ cup rock salt
- 1 cup fresh mint (finely chopped)
- 1 cup fresh bay leaves (finely chopped)
- 1 teaspoon coconut oil
- 1 teaspoon almond oil
- Mesh bag or cheesecloth

How to make it:

1. Mix all ingredients together and place in the mesh bag
2. Put the bag under your running bath water
3. Get in the bath and enjoy the lovely herbal infusion

Deep Soak Bath Salts

What you need:

- 1 ½ cups sea salt
- ½ cup baking powder
- 3 tablespoons sweet almond oil
- 2 teaspoons apricot kernel
- 2 teaspoons avocado oil
- 5 drops sandalwood essential oil
- 5 drops rosewood essential oil
- 5 drops ylang ylang essential oil
- 5 drops chamomile essential oil
- Air tight jar

How to make it:

1. Put all ingredients in the air tight jar and shake vigorously to combine all ingredients
2. Make sure they are mixed together well
3. Allow the scents to infuse by leaving it to sit for 2 hours
4. Add to your running bath and enjoy

Ocean Fresh Bath Salts

What you need:

- 1 ½ cups sea salt
- 1 cup Epsom salts
- 4 drops blue food coloring
- 3 drops jasmine essential oil
- 4 drops vanilla
- 2 tablespoons glycerin
- Air tight jar

How to make it:

1. Put all ingredients in the air tight jar and shake vigorously to combine all ingredients
2. Make sure they are mixed together well
3. Allow the scents to infuse by leaving it to sit for 2 hours
4. Add to your running bath and enjoy

Citrus Bath Salts

What you need:

- ½ cup baking soda
- ¼ cup Epsom salts
- ¼ teaspoon orange fragrance oil
- ¼ teaspoon tangerine fragrance oil
- 2 drops liquid food coloring (any color you like)
- Air tight jar

How to make it:

1. Put all ingredients in the air tight jar and shake vigorously to combine all ingredients
2. Make sure they are mixed together well
3. Allow the scents to infuse by leaving it to sit for 2 hours
4. Add to your running bath and enjoy

Pretty Peach Bath Salts

What you need:

- 1 ½ cups sea salt
- 1 cup Epsom salts
- ½ cup baking soda
- 10 drops peach fragrance oil
- 10 drops bergamot essential oil
- 7 drops vanilla essential oil
- 3 drops orange essential oil
- Air tight jar

How to make it:

1. Put all ingredients in the air tight jar and shake vigorously to combine all ingredients
2. Make sure they are mixed together well
3. Allow the scents to infuse by leaving it to sit for 2 hours
4. Add to your running bath and enjoy

Uplifting Bath Salts

What you need:

- 1 cup Epsom salt
- 1 tablespoon baking soda
- 1 cup rock salt
- 4 drops peppermint essential oil
- 2 drops rosemary essential oil
- 2 drops lavender essential oil
- 2 drops rose essential oil
- Air tight jar

How to make it:

1. Put all ingredients in the air tight jar and shake vigorously to combine all ingredients
2. Make sure they are mixed together well
3. Allow the scents to infuse by leaving it to sit for 2 hours
4. Add to your running bath and enjoy

Heavy Head Bath Salts

What you need:

- 1 cup Epsom salt
- 1 tablespoon baking soda
- 1 cup rock salt
- 4 drops peppermint essential oil
- 8 drops eucalyptus essential oil
- Air tight jar

How to make it:

1. Put all ingredients in the air tight jar and shake vigorously to combine all ingredients
2. Make sure they are mixed together well
3. Allow the scents to infuse by leaving it to sit for 2 hours
4. Add to your running bath and enjoy

Lemongrass & Cinnamon Bath Salts

What you need:

- 1 cup sea salt
- 3 tablespoons baking soda
- 5 drops lemongrass essential oil
- 5 drops cinnamon essential oil
- Air tight jar

How to make it:

1. Put all ingredients in the air tight jar and shake vigorously to combine
2. Make sure they are mixed together well
3. Allow the scents to infuse by leaving it to sit for 2 hours
4. Add to your running bath and enjoy

Lemon Fizz Bath Salts

What you need:

- 1 cup sea salt
- 3 tablespoons baking soda
- 2 tablespoons citric acid
- 10 drops lemon essential oil
- Air tight jar

How to make it:

1. Put all ingredients in the air tight jar and shake vigorously to combine
2. Make sure they are mixed together well
3. Allow the scents to infuse by leaving it to sit for 2 hours
4. Add to your running bath and enjoy

Toxin Exterminator Bath Salts

What you need:

- 1 cup sea salt
- ½ cup rock salt
- 3 drops basil essential oil
- 3 drops grapefruit essential oil
- 3 drops juniper essential oil
- 2 drops lemon essential oil
- Air tight jar

How to make it:

1. Put all ingredients in the air tight jar and shake vigorously to combine
2. Make sure they are mixed together well
3. Allow the scents to infuse by leaving it to sit for 2 hours
4. Add to your running bath and enjoy

Bubble Baths

You can't beat a long lovely bath where you can soak your aching muscles and relax in total comfort. With a few candles, soft music and the right bubble bath, you can be forgiven for thinking you are in a top hotel spa. Use the recipes in this section to create this feeling yourself at home for a fraction of the price.

Depending on the quality of the oils, liquid soap and fragrances you use, you can create some amazing bubble bath recipes. The benefits of these homemade pampering products are plenty. Try a few, you will be hooked!

A few notes:

- These bubble baths are so easy to make, there's no need making more than you need, that way it stays fresh and you get maximum benefits from the properties of the ingredients used
- You can add dried herbs and flowers to your bubble bath to add interest
- You can mix and match the oils and herbs that I use, use what you like, it is your recipe.
- Experiment with different ingredients and enjoy yourself.

Cherry Bubble Bath

What you need:

- ½ cup unscented shampoo
- ¾ cup water
- ½ teaspoon table salt
- 15 drops cherry fragrance oil
- Bottle for storage

How to make it:

1. Pour shampoo in a bowl and add the water
2. Stir until mixed together well
3. Add the salt and stir until the mixture thickens a bit
4. Add cherry fragrance oil and mix again
5. Pour it into the bottle
6. Add it to your bath as and when you feel like it
7. Relax and enjoy

Bergamot & Lime Bubble Bath

What you need:

- 8 oz. liquid soap
- 2 oz. distilled water
- 7 drops bergamot essential oil
- 5 drops lime essential oil
- 3 drops vanilla fragrance oil
- 2 drops gardenia fragrance oil
- ¾ cup water
- ½ teaspoon table salt
- 15 drops cherry fragrance oil
- Bottle for storage

How to make it:

1. Pour all ingredients into the bottle and shake vigorously to mix together well
2. Add it to your bath as and when you feel like it
3. Relax and enjoy this luxury bubble bath

Lavender Bubble Bath

What you need:

- 5 drops lavender essential oil
- 1 quart water
- 1 bar castile soap
- 1 ½ oz. glycerin
- Bottle or container for storage

How to make it:

1. Grate the bar of soap into a bowl
2. Add the remaining ingredients
3. Pour the mixture into the bottle or container and mix well
4. Add it to your bath as and when you feel like it

Honey & Vanilla Bubble Bath

What you need:

- 1 cup olive oil
- ½ cup liquid soap
- ¼ cup honey
- 1 tablespoon vanilla extract
- ½ teaspoon table salt
- 15 drops cherry fragrance oil
- Bottle for storage

How to make it:

1. Blend all ingredients together until well combined
2. Pour into your bottle
3. Add it to your bath as and when you feel like it
4. Relax and enjoy this luxury bubble bath

Rosemary Milk Bath

I What you need:

- 2 cups dry milk powder
- 1 cup cornstarch
- 2 teaspoons fresh rosemary
- Bottle for storage

How to make it:

1. Mix the milk powder and cornstarch together and mix well
2. Add the fresh rosemary
3. Pour it into your bottle and shake vigorously
4. Add it to your bath as and when you feel like it
5. Relax and enjoy this luxury bubble bath

Milk & Honey Bubble Bath

What you need:

- ½ cup dry milk powder
- ½ cup honey
- ¼ cup olive oil
- Bottle for storage

How to make it:

1. Pour all ingredients into the bottle and shake vigorously to mix together well
2. Add it to your bath as and when you feel like it
3. Relax and enjoy this luxury bubble bath

Raspberry Bubble Bath

What you need:

- 8 oz. liquid soap
- 2 oz. distilled water
- 7 drops raspberry fragrance oil
- 8 drops vanilla fragrance oil
- 2 drops red liquid food coloring
- Bottle for storage

How to make it:

1. Pour all ingredients into the bottle and shake vigorously to mix together well
2. Add it to your bath as and when you feel like it
3. Relax and enjoy this luxury bubble bath

Rose Bubble Bath

What you need:

- 1 bar castile soap (grated)
- 3 ounces glycerin
- 1 quart water
- 5 drops rose essential oil
- Bottle for storage

How to make it:

1. Pour all ingredients into the bottle and shake vigorously to mix together well
2. Add it to your bath as and when you feel like it
3. Relax and enjoy this luxury bubble bath

Herb & Oil Bubble Bath

What you need:

- 4 teaspoons fresh rosemary (or any herb you like)
- 8 drops lemon essential oil
- 1 cup distilled water
- 1 cup liquid soap
- Bottle for storage

How to make it:

1. In a small pan, bring the water and herbs to a boil
2. Allow it to simmer for 30 minutes in order to infuse the scents
3. Let it cool and squeeze the rosemary leaves to release the extra aroma
4. Combine this mixture to the liquid soap and essential oils
5. Pour into your bottle
6. Add it to your bath as and when you feel like it
7. Relax and enjoy this luxury bubble bath

Jasmine Delight Bubble Bath

What you need:

- 3 drops rose fragrance oil
- 3 drops Jasmine fragrance oil
- 1 ounce glycerine
- 1 ounce coconut oil
- 1 bar castile soap (grated)
- 1 quart water
- Bottle for storage

How to make it:

1. Pour all ingredients into the bottle and shake vigorously to mix together well
2. Add it to your bath as and when you feel like it
3. Relax and enjoy this luxury bubble bath

Apple Bubble Bath

What you need:

- 5 drops green apple fragrance oil
- 1 quart water
- 1 bar castile soap (grated)
- 1 ½ ounces glycerine
- 5 drops green liquid food coloring (optional)
- Bottle for storage

How to make it:

1. Pour all ingredients into the bottle and shake vigorously to mix together well
2. Add it to your bath as and when you feel like it
3. Relax and enjoy this luxury bubble bath

Conclusion

Well there you have it, **53** of the best recipes I know for making bath bombs, bath salts & bubble bath. Now go and create some of these yourself and put your own unique recipes together as well.

Remember, you are not only adding these wonderful natural ingredients to your bathing routine because they smell nice, you are adding these ingredients and putting them on your skin because of the enormous amount of moisturizing and health benefits associated with the particular oils and herbs too. Natural products are simply the best things you can use on your skin.

You really owe it to yourself to pamper your body and give yourself the opportunity to have lots of relaxing and meditating baths. The recipes in this book will help you to achieve just that. They will encourage you to spend time with yourself.

I do hope you enjoy the recipes in this book. If you could, I would really appreciate it if you could leave me a review for the book. This will help others to get a feeling about the contents and will also hopefully encourage them to experiment with their own homemade natural organic bathing products too.

Thanks for reading

Lorraine Xx

Don't Forget To Check Out My Other Books in This Series

Homemade Body Scrubs : 52 All Natural And Easy To Make Body Scrubs, Face Masks, Lip Balms And Body Washes

Homemade Lotion : 41 All Natural Simple And Easy To Make Body Lotions, Body Butters and Lotion Bars

How To Be Beautiful With Homemade Beauty Products. Over 50 Organic Face Masks, Face Cleansers & Face Creams

Homemade Shampoo: Make Your Own Organic & Natural Hair Products For Luscious Hair

Homemade Foot Spa: 48 All Natural Foot Soak, Foot Scrubs, Foot Creams & Heel Balm Recipes

Homemade Deodorant: 32 Simple Organic DIY Recipes For Making Natural Deodorants & Body Sprays

Printed in Great Britain
by Amazon

79834357R00041